MW01070932

At Play in the Garden of Stitch

thoughts that come while eyeing the needle

Paula Kovarik

Yellow Brick Studio Press

No part of this book may be reproduced in any form or by
any other means without the written consent of Paula Kovarik.
Inquiries should be addressed to Paula Kovarik at
atplayinthegardenofstitch@gmail.com
or 1957 Jackson Ave., Memphis, TN 38107.

Library of Congress Cataloging-in-Publication Data

Kovarik, Paula
At Play in the Garden of Stitch
Summary: thoughts that come while eyeing the needle

ISBN: 978-0-578-92004-7

for Lorraine

Welcome to my playroom

I was talking to a friend the other day about journals. I had unearthed a box of memorabilia from my high school and college days. I spent the day looking at yearbooks, journals and old photos. I sorted, culled and discarded the extraneous. I was left with a pile that was just too hard to categorize. What exactly do you do with those things?

And then I started to think about my art. Piles and bins and shelves of raw materials clog my studio. I have things hanging in the hallways, dangling from ceilings and hidden in drawers. When I look at this studio shot, it proves that I expand to fill the space available. My studio used to be an extra sitting room off our bedroom. Now it takes up a whole building.

My work as an artist reflects this studio. My art is an amalgam of my thoughts and experiences. Since working full time as an artist, I am flooded with even more ideas to pursue. I am itchy and eager to create.

This book too is an amalgam, and it includes several different types of messages. I'll tell you about how I work and think as I make new quilts. I'll have several stories of particular quilts, what they're about and how I made them. I'll include a few "photo album" essays taken from my online journal (paulakovarik.com/journal) that give an insight into how my life experiences continue to influence my art. And, for those of you with an adventurous spirit, I'll include some simple exercises to spur practice in your own studio.

So, welcome to my collection of thoughts, insights and exercises. I'm glad you're here.

Clutter is the precursor to clarity.

What to know

Having an art practice means you have to practice. A lot. It means that you have to be honest with yourself as well as your medium. You have to know what that medium does under pressure, and what you do when you are under pressure. You have to consider what motivates you. You have to be curious, willing to fail, optimistic about results and happy to spend the time.

You have to practice.

You have to make a mess.

You have to feel the depth.

Then try again.

I've been stitching for over 15 years. I take it seriously, but I also recognize that it is only practice. The act of stitching reveals my inner thoughts and drives me to new discoveries. The process of making art is more important to me than the final product. That's why I always say: **It's process, not product.** I live in that zone that makes me want to search more. Feel more. Say more.

I chose the quilted form in my art for its versatility, intimacy and depth. Using cloth as a structural element for composition brings texture and a physical presence to my work. The main focus of my work has been what comes next: intricate free-motion stitching that animates the surface of the cloth, to express my thoughts and emotions.

The exercises in this book focus on this style of free-motion stitching and how you can use it in your own art. I hope this book inspires you to find new ways to practice. Practice doesn't always make perfect, but it does improve the product.

In the Deep, 37" x 35", detail, 2019

My toolbox

This simple list gives me a starting point for the **PRACTICE** of my art. Practicing brings insight, success and failure. If you want to play along, you'll need to assemble these materials:

- A way to capture images: digital camera, computer tablet, smartphone
- A sewing machine with the ability to do free-motion quilting. A free-motion quilting foot is essential. I prefer the ones that are plastic and transparent.
- Sewing notions, including straight pins, hand-stitching and self-threading needles, scissors and a seam ripper
- Machine quilting needles, size 12 quilting, 14 topstitch and 16 topstitch
- Black cotton fabric cut into 14" squares
- Ivory or white cotton fabric cut into 14" squares
- Cotton backing fabric, (any color or pattern) cut into 14" squares
- Batting: a variety to test
- Thread: Three spools, one each of black, white and variegated black-to-white

- One extra fine tip dry erase marker in black
- One sheet of clear acetate, 14" x 17"
- Chalk marker (a Clover product shown above at far left), white
- Fons and Porter mechanical fabric pencils, white and black
- Journal, legal pad or diary to keep notes

Thread, fabric and batting

I use YLI brand thread almost exclusively, but have also been satisfied with the King Tut line of Superior Threads. Both brands are developed for machine quilting and are 40 wt., 100% long staple cotton. A 50 wt. thread—the standard all-purpose sewing thread—is too subtle for these illustrative techniques.

I like the Robert Kaufman line of Kona cotton fabrics. The cotton is densely woven and holds its shape well after stitching. I use a cotton batting with it, sometimes a double layer if I want extra loft.

Lately I have been using untreated canvas for my work. With canvas, or other heavier fabric such as upholstery weight cloth, I use a loftier batting such as wool so it shows depth when stitched.

Found fabrics such as napkins, tablecloths and clothing summon me with their tears and stains to transform them. The stains speak of former use.

Experimenting with different fabrics and batting is part of my process. I will often do a couple of test strips to find exactly how I want the piece to work.

With batting I tend to stick with natural fibers like wool, cotton or silk. I like how they can transform the surface when washed. You may have your own favorite fabric and batting, or you may want to test out many kinds and see what you like. Make notes on your samples of what you use so you can refer to them for future projects.

To begin

I look for ways to communicate my ideas and emotions. The fabric acts as a canvas, the thread as a pen. Here's the way I approach my work:

- **First, make a mess.** Approach each day with a curious mind willing to make a mess of expectations. No mistakes.

- **Embrace the wonky.** Make the most of whatever occurs by letting the thread lead. No regrets.

- **Think in thread.** Make careful observations of the world for an unlimited number of pathways to pursue. No limits.

- **Chart a new path.** Work out solutions by using composition, layering and experimentation. No dead ends.

One trick

A piece of acetate to play with line

One of the most challenging parts of free-motion quilting is figuring out where and what you will stitch. I use a simple technique that helps me visualize different patterns before I commit to them with thread.

Using a large piece of acetate and a dry erase marker, I sketch my ideas onto the acetate directly over the quilt. I can move the acetate around to experiment with placement of a motif or pattern. If I don't like the first pattern I can simply wipe it dry and start again. Though the drawn lines are thicker than a stitched line would be, they give me an idea of how I might proceed. Drawing these lines trains my hands and brain in a trial run for the real deal.

Once I have decided what I want to do, I mark a boundary for the pattern on the quilt with a chalk marker. My favorite of these has a roller at the tip that makes a thin dotted line with chalk. You can get white, blue, yellow and pink chalk. Stick with the white stuff. The other colors can stain your fabric.

I'll often hang the acetate near my machine so that I can see it while stitching. I'll do this stitching in the morning when I am fresher.

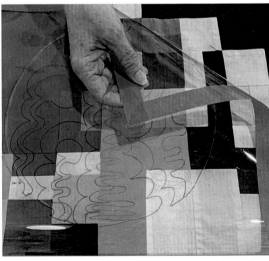

Laying the acetate sheet over my composition gives me a safe space to experiment with lines. Those squiggly lines I have drawn on the acetate represent what I might stitch on the actual composition.

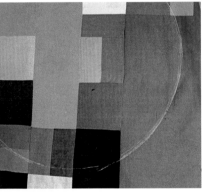

Drawing a rough chalk line gives me a guide for where I want to stitch. The chalk brushes off easily.

Using your acetate

A sheet of acetate is a wondrous thing. You can use it to make drawings with dry erase markers. You can trace pictures of things you want to incorporate into your work. And, you can change your mind without reaching for the seam ripper to take out stitches.

Try this. Draw a line on your acetate over one of your quilt blocks. Move it around. Change its direction. Repeat it 10 times. Take a picture; erase; try a new kind of line. Try drawing a repeat motif such as a flower or a series of circles. Then decide which of these best complements your piecing and reinforces your meaning.

Add this tool to your toolbox and reach for it every time you have questions about what to do next.

A word of warning

Add a strip of tape to the edges of the acetate so that you don't inadvertently draw over the edge onto the cloth below. Ask me how I know that.

First, see it

Recording the things I see as inspirations is a daily practice. Ever since the invention of the cellphone camera, this task has become easier. I consciously look for details in landscapes, connections in collections and energy in the lines that define our world. Using these simple snapshots for stitching paths gives me a way to explore line in my own way rather than following someone else's patterns.

Then, remember it

I don't draw on my fabric with any type of marker, but I do draw on paper prior to experimenting with new ideas for stitching. I find that it helps my hands remember what the line will do when I start stitching. Office paper works, but you can also add your line experiments to a bound journal or computer archive to keep for reference.

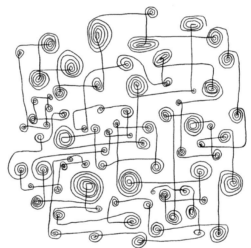

Now, stitch it

This one-line stitching pattern has infinite possibilities. I experiment with scale, color and shape. Many quilters follow the quilt police "rule" about never crossing lines. For me, crossing lines allows me to travel wherever I want to on the surface without the worry of keeping an eye on void spaces.

Take it for a spin. It is a lot of fun. Practice spirals and circles on one of your 14" squares so that you will feel comfortable doing them on a final piece.

stitch tip

Spiral paths

When working with spirals, do not twirl your fabric. Instead develop the skill to make the spiral while keeping your fabric horizon the same. In other words, sometimes you will be stitching sideways, sometimes backward and sometimes forward. You'll find that stitching in some directions is harder than others, and your line will be wonkier, but that will just make your spiral more fun to look at.

The same goes for stitching circles or other closed spaces. Keep the fabric pointing in the same direction while stitching round and round.

Linestorming

stitch tip

Feed dogs up, needle down

When stitching with a free-motion foot, I do not lower the feed dogs on my machine. Instead I leave them up and move a little slower to feel the pull against the fabric.

I also use the needle down position on my machine so that when I pause, my fabric sandwich will not shift position. Pausing with the needle down allows me to consider design changes. If I'm stitching corners, that rest stop lets me think about which way to turn.

Line attributes			
smooth	fast	zigzag	circular
winding	crazy	curly	bumpy
carefree	surprising	jittery	angry
spiraling	rectilinear	swirling	floral

To begin

Assemble your materials. You'll need some paper, a fine line pen, and quilt sandwiches for this exercise. Put together your 14" quilt sandwiches using one layer of solid color, one layer of batting and one layer of backing fabric. There is no need to baste them together. I like to create the sandwiches in quantity so that they are ready when I feel like experimenting.

First draw

1. **Take out some paper and your fine line pen.** Any paper will do.

2. **Visualize active and emotional lines.** Consider the words in the table above. Think about how each attribute would look if it were a line.

   Now draw them. Do this quickly with an intuitive flair. Experiment with criss-crossing the lines to create shape or pattern. Repeat or echo a line to see how it builds a pattern. Try each attribute on a separate piece of paper or combine two attributes on a page.

Repeating a line will change the texture of your quilt sandwich.

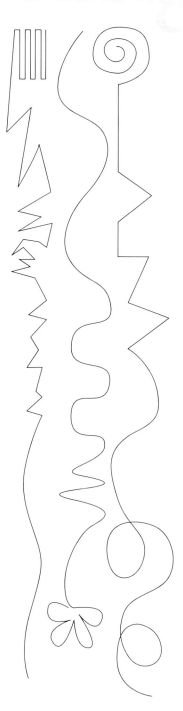

Changing the attribute of a line can give the viewer some clues about the story you are telling.

Then stitch

1. **Prepare your sewing machine with a contrasting thread.** If you start with a black fabric sandwich, use white thread and vice versa. Attach your free-motion foot.

2. **Divide your first quilt sandwich into quarters.** Score the fabric with a ruler or use a chalk line to divide the space.

3. **Referencing your line drawings, fill each quarter of your square with a different type of line.** Try filling the area without rotating your fabric. Sometimes you will be stitching forward and other times backward, sometimes left, other times right.

Thread lines create textural guideposts that move the eye across a quilted piece. Density adds flatness. Swirls add action and lines point to important sections.

Finally, build a story

1. **Start a new quilt sandwich.** Divide your square in half by scoring a line with a straight edge or chalk line.

2. **Choose two or three different attributes of line and combine them in one continuous line.** A line may start out smooth but then move toward jittery as the line travels.

3. **Fill half of the square with that line** traveling and reacting to itself. Try it again on the other side with a different type of line.

Rhythm in your composition adds a dynamic beat. If you repeat a line over and over with the same attributes you create a stabilizing factor to the texture of the piece. If you vary the line, the eye hops or stops at that variation. Control how the eye moves across your piece by adding rest stops or dynamic peaks.

Warming up exercises can loosen you up before tackling a work in progress. Always have a practice square at the side of your work area that you can stitch with gusto. The practice square can also be used to test tension when changing threads.

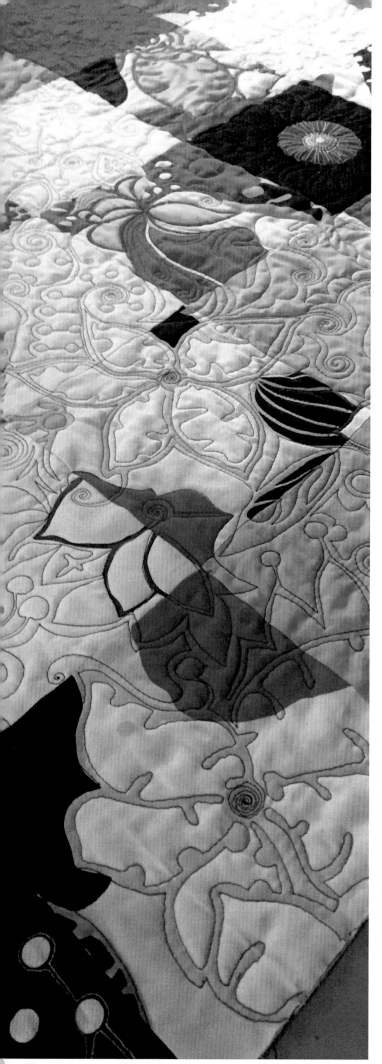

Reactive stitching

Learning to react can be as simple as repeating motifs or building on the vocabulary that is already in your fabric. Intersperse solid fabrics with patterned pieces to show-case your stitching.

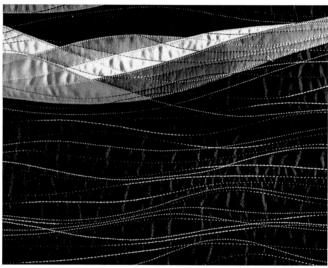

Repeating the curving lines of this construction adds action to the waves of color.

The large circular area in the middle of this piece appears because of the stitching, not because of the patchwork itself.

Each one of these quadrants speaks a different language.

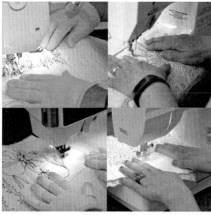

Some wear gloves, some do not. I like them, because they allow for a better grip with less pressure, and therefore are kinder to the wrists. Quilting gloves can be found in fabric stores. Look for ones with a plasticized tread on the fingertips.

Notice how that empty circle becomes the focal point in this stitching sample. Creating rest stops for the eye brings ideas into focus.

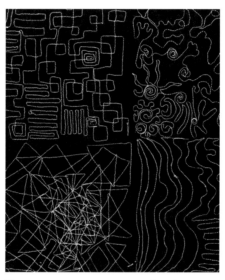

Yes, you can cross over your lines!

Shattering lines add action and emphasize fault lines in this composition. The lines tell the same story as the pieced fabric.

Think about how densely you are stitching. Do lines that are closer together pull your eyes to that detail?

stitch tip

Learning to react

Paul Klee once said that "a line is a dot that went for a walk." The line you stitch is a path that reacts to what is already there. If there is a pattern in your fabric, you can mimic it. If there are two types of patterns next to each other, you can link them. If you want to unify a surface, you can add a repeating textural pattern over the entire surface. In all cases your stitching is reacting to what is already there, while also showing your emotions, mood and thoughts.

Stop thinking Start stitching

It's easy to be distracted by the rest of the stuff going on outside the studio—disturbing news stories, health or financial worries, children demanding an afternoon snack or help with homework, the noise from the construction project next door. Turn it off. Turn off the social media and the TV. Close the door. Put on some music that you love. Take out the sketch book and scribble.

Start with a what if

For instance, what if you only used straight lines and angular corners when drawing a line that never ended? Fill up the page, then turn it 90 degrees to fill it up again.

On to stitching

What good is a drawing without a little thread and fabric? Take out one of your 14" fabric sandwiches to start the game.

It's all about commitment

This exercise will stop you thinking about anything but where the thread wants to go. You have to anticipate the turns.

Next step? Fill in the blanks. This step is like finding treasure. Filling in spaces defines new shapes. The stitched fill meanders across the surface animating negative and positive shapes.

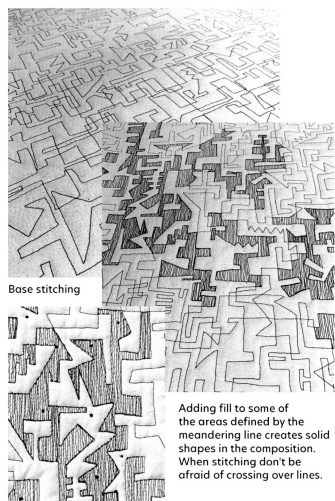

Base stitching

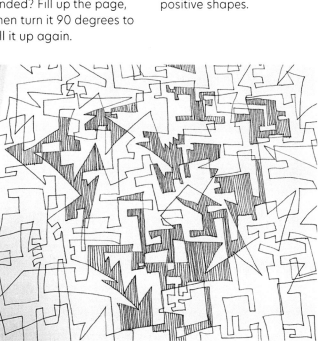

Your drawing gives you a starting point for how the needle will move.

Most days, I brush aside distractions to focus on a pattern or a piece. Immersing myself in the process allows my inner thoughts to float to the surface.

Adding fill to some of the areas defined by the meandering line creates solid shapes in the composition. When stitching don't be afraid of crossing over lines.

What do you see?

Shapes can define buildings, animals, abstractions or, in the case of this example, some abstract faces. Adding stitched dots to the surface brings some of the shapes to life.

I make these dots with my free-motion foot. Place your needle where you want a dot, bring up the bottom thread to avoid thread nests and stitch while wiggling the fabric in tiny circles until your dot is as big as you want it to be. Then, clip the threads and move on to your next dot.

Fluidity

With practice you will develop a feel for the area in which it is most comfortable for you to stitch. A lot will depend on what type of machine you are using and how you support the fabric with your sewing table. The larger the harp or throat of your machine and the more area you have around the machine to keep the fabric flat, the more area you can stitch comfortably.

Stitching without twirling or re-positioning the fabric sandwich can be more playful. If you have to stop and move the fabric it can constrain the line.

Sometimes it is impossible to keep your quilt sandwich positioned so that you can stitch fluidly. Then, stop with the needle down, rearrange your quilt sandwich and start again.

practice

Scribble and fill

Get out some blank paper and a black pen, and scribble your heart away—no bounds or expectations. Make up your own *what if* question. It could be *what if I draw a series of looping lines*, or *what if I make all turns in my line at 90 degrees*, or *what if all my lines are zigzags*. Fill your paper with a line that answers that question, then choose some areas to fill with a different pattern. In the case above I used a straight line fill that brought all of those negative areas together. Then get out one of your practice squares and do it in thread.

Fenceposts

Filling a space with a repeat pattern creates a bumpy regularity. Lots of traditional quilts use this technique over the entire surface of a quilt. The implied grid—made by the structural lines—holds it all together.

In this technique the pattern is made by stitching up and down that implied grid.

While traveling along the line, you are reacting to what came before. You can alternate the shapes, change the size of the shapes, or repeat the shapes in orderly conformity.

Try this:

1. **Start in one corner** of your square and stitch a line that has bumps in it.

2. **Return to the beginning** and complete the shapes you have created in the first line on the way back.

3. **Turn the corner** and do it again but this time stagger the shapes so that you fill in the gridded post. Continue to fill the square with your pattern.

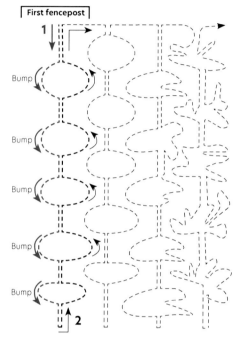

First fencepost

Bump
Bump
Bump
Bump
Bump

This example shows the difference between butting the shapes next to each other and staggering the shapes. Both methods create strong patterns.

Reactive stitching and the role of pattern in the work

Using a pattern to direct the eye across a quilt adds texture and order to the quilt surface. The pattern acts as a unifier for the piece. We search for pattern and order naturally. When the order is disrupted, we notice.

Varying the shapes in the fenceposts can add an element of syncopation to the surface. Use a variegated thread and the pattern may appear and disappear.

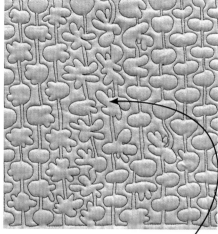

Changing the shape in this textural pattern automatically focuses the eye on that area.

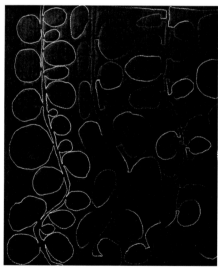

Look at the difference in the pattern when using a solid contrasting thread as opposed to using a variegated thread. The pattern appears and disappears with the variegated thread.

Fenceposts don't have to be straight.

This grouping shows a flair for variety. Those "bumps" can be anything you want.

Adding eyes to these fencepost shapes makes this composition look like a wild party.

Varying the size of the shapes adds focal points and density.

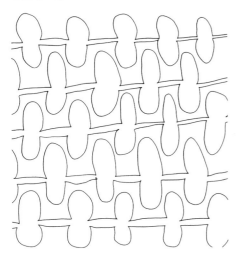

Doing a simple circle pattern and then turning it 90 degrees to repeat the pattern produces a riot of intersecting shapes.

Draw or stitch?

Both! Practicing the fencepost technique with pen and paper is a good way to develop hand and eye memory when starting to stitch. Practice this technique by drawing a line with bumps on one side and then mimic the bumps on the way back to the beginning. You could choose to make all the bumps the same or, as in some of the drawings shown here, you could morph them into other shapes.

Then try stitching your pattern to see how it changes the surface of your quilt. If the shapes are all the same size the pattern will have a uniform bumpy texture. If the shapes change in size you can create centers of interest.

The piece on the left was done using the fencepost technique. The technique can be used without repeating a pattern. I started on the center spiral (see the red lines that illustrate parts of my pathway) and moved up and down the quilt. After finishing the line work I drew a faint line with my pencil for the circular shapes and I filled the shapes with thread.

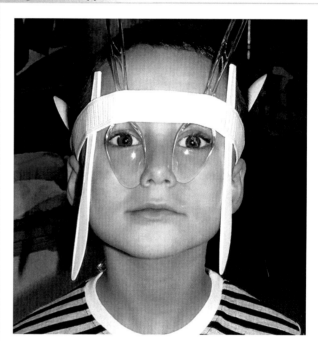

Focusing the lens

Many people work in series. I have done a number of pieces that look similar to the piece on the left. But mostly I work like a taste tester. The horizon contains a spectrum of possibilities. Those little flickering lights of ideas challenge me to focus the lens.

Inspiration is rocky. The ride is bumpy. The point is to keep going. It can be as simple as a line attribute or as difficult as climate change. Each project has a list of ingredients, insights and aims. Each requires weeding out the extraneous, simplifying the knotty and, sometimes, adding depth where no bottom is seen.

Now, let me clean my glasses and get on with it.

Pathways, 27.5" x 28", detail, 2019

Working in series

Using the fencepost technique gives me a way to get lost in stitch. It's like a meditation.

Here's another quilt in the Pathways series. I move up and down the piece, filling in spaces as I go along. I have developed my own vocabulary of stitched shapes that repeat in all of my work—arrows, faces, birds, trees, monsters, stars and squares and circles.

When I approach a piece like this I am simply meandering across its surface. If I feel like adding a dog I add a dog, if I want to add a monster I find a place for a monster. I might stitch one half of a flower shape and then come back to it on the down stroke to finish the other half.

I could choose to do the entire surface in dogs. But I like the variety that this playground gives me.

What shapes will you develop over time?

Pathways II, **38" x 23", detail, 2019. Following these pathways may make you dizzy.**

From the collection of Linda Ober

On expectations

Recently, my son unearthed my case of Barbie clothes from the attic. I don't remember playing with this doll.

My Aunt Emmie provided most of the clothing for this doll with her expert knitting. I'm amazed at her skill now, though I didn't admire that skill then. We took it for granted. She had a thing for pink.

All the essentials of a 60s girl were there:

☑ little black dress

☑ lacy underwear

☑ apron

☑ wedding dress

☑ house dress

☑ pocketbooks

The clothes gave us a map of expectations.

I see by the rat's nest of hair that dear Barbie went through some tough times. She ditched the three-piece red knit outfit for a mini-skirt and tights.

There are no professional clothes or workshop gloves. There is no briefcase, no computer. Yet there are two aprons, one practical with a matching chef's hat and one frilly to greet her husband upon his return home. I do love to cook.

It's a box of propaganda that made sense to the executives at Mattel at the time. I've heard that Barbie has evolved over time with scuba gear, ski togs and business attire. At the time, we tried on these women's uniforms to suit society's norms. We told these sto-ries to each other through dating games, house play and dress-up. We learned how to walk in heels, put on makeup and wish upon a star. There is probably a version of this narrative out there for girls under 16 to this day.

A little box of expectations.

I followed a different path. I grew up during a time of questioning authority—a time when women fought for equal rights, a time when civil discourse turned to difficult subjects. The subjects are getting even more difficult now. Our planet, our rights, our nations, our health—all at risk.

So when I look at this little box of expectations I am thinking about how we're still swimming upstream in a one-piece bathing suit, constrained by expectations. We'll need to add some armor to the closet. We'll need resilience and a fierce belief in each other. We'll need to put on our big girl pants and stand up, move forward and speak out loud.

Now where did I put that rotary cutter?

Do your childhood dreams match the reality of your life? Did you ever envision your life as you find it now?

One day, while out and about, Mom asked a biker if she could sit on his motorcycle. I wondered if she was going to start it up and ride away.

Then and now

I had a very supportive mother. She taught me everything she knew. Knitting, crocheting, sewing, gardening, cooking, camping, baiting a hook, standing up for myself, taking responsibility for my actions, dreaming without limits. She was a nurse, a community organizer and a cheerleader for each of her children.

She taught my brothers and me to navigate by stopping the car, turning to one of us and asking for directions home. She would follow our directions regardless of whether they were correct or not. Then, if hopelessly lost, she would ask what steps we should take to get to our destination. We learned not to panic, to always notice landmarks and to develop our own inner compass by observing the sun.

She taught me about confidence, consequences and community. She laughed more often than she cried. I channel her all the time when I make decisions about my work. Her voice is in my mind as I flounder. It is to her that I want to show my progress.

thoughts from my journal

Invisible

We all feel it sometimes—that feeling that nobody really sees who we are. It's as if we are invisible.

Inside, it all makes sense. Thoughts line up with values. Insights are gilded with experience. Ideas careen through our minds with possibility and hope.

I was lucky. I grew up being taught that I could be anything I wanted to be. My experiences have taught me to use my own vision to explore the depths of meaning in my life.

As an older woman, I am invisible to many. Little do they know that I ride hot rod wheels on the many-splendored roads of life.

Invisible, 20" x 20" x 57", 2020

Heroes

Storytellers create narratives. They have control over what is seen and what is hidden. They lead the audience through a series of clues for the resolution of a plot. Storytellers create heroes.

The same can be said of stitching. Through color, composition and line, the stitcher directs the eye to the story parts of a piece. Some areas become heroes, others supporting characters.

Try this exercise to create your own heroes.

1. **Set up a new quilt sandwich.** Choose black or white fabric and a contrasting thread.

2. **Outline a void.** With chalk or light pencil draw some areas within your square that will receive no thread.

3. **Stitch to avoid.** Starting on the outside edge of your sandwich stitch to the void area. Then return to the edge of the piece. Use a simple line fill as in the sample below or a more complicated fencepost fill. When you come to the void area, you will need to travel on its edge or back to the beginning. Notice how the void areas are not outlined in stitch, only implied by the stitching that surrounds them.

4. **Change the line attribute.** Another way to define a hero is to travel to the chalked outline and then change the line attribute within it, as in the samples on the facing page.

Heroes are focal points in your composition. In this example, the void area within the stitching is a hero or main character of the composition. All eyes focus there.

In the cacophony that is our society, I am always happy to find a space to think. It is the luxury of silence.

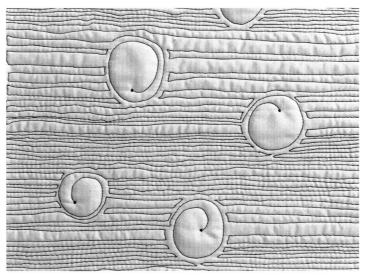

Notice how my lines are very wonky and inconsistent? That is purposeful on my part. I like the way they ripple the surface of the cloth. If your lines are wiggly and rippling, try making them even more wiggly. Or try to make them ruler straight and see how that affects the look of the piece.

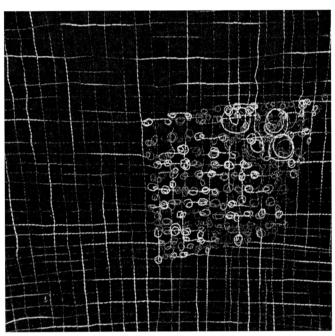

Curly stitches and a gridded background define the hero in this piece. Moving your quilt sandwich in tight circles under the needle can create this curly texture.

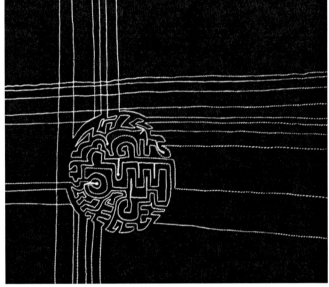

The ball of geometric stitches seems to float above this simple background.

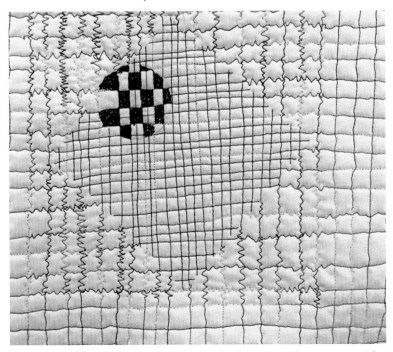

Notice how this artist uses variegated thread to create the nervous grid that leads to the center hero. The pattern appears and disappears to create a tension within.

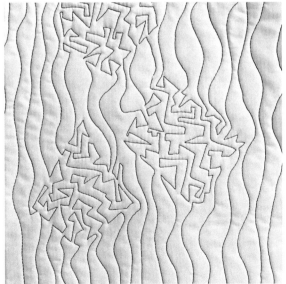

Instead of avoiding the areas defined by chalk, fill them with a contrasting line attribute. These smooth lines erupt into a geometric pattern within the chalked outline.

This stitching bursts with energy. In stitching, density flattens the quilt sandwich and adds detail.

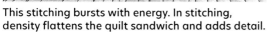

The heroes on this page show how versatile this technique can be.

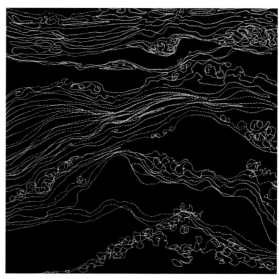

Those areas without stitch can be as powerful as the areas with stitch.

This delightful fish is swimming in deep space. The contrast between his curved lines and the straight line fill behind him adds to the sense of depth.

These curved lines focus all of their energy on the void within.

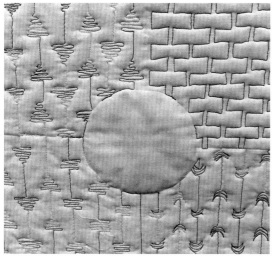

These stitched patterns define a hero by creating a space with no stitching.

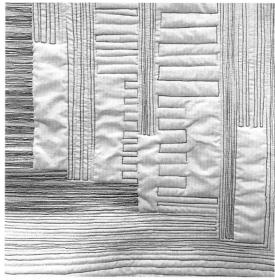

Changing the density of the stitching in this piece yields hero shapes where there are no stitches.

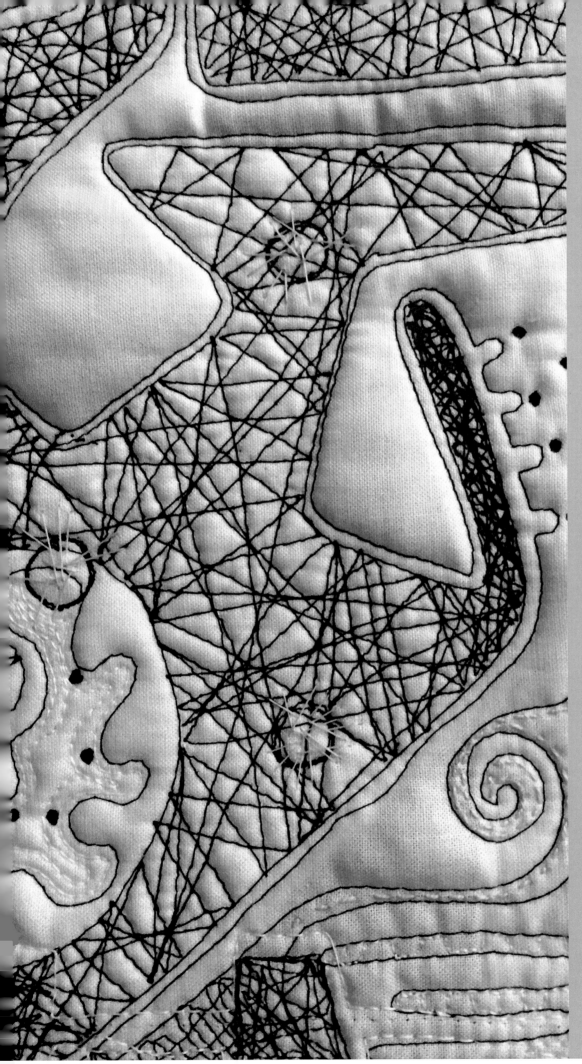

stitch tip

Heroes and fills

In this quilt, I cut some random shapes from red fabric and put them between the batting and the ivory top fabric while making the quilt sandwich. The red fabric tinted the top layer and provided warmer coloring in the composition. It also gave me a vague outline for the heroes in the composition. Adding hand stitching brought life to the inanimate objects. Playing with dense fills activated the negative spaces and flattened the area around the heroes.

When you work on a composition, think about how you can reinforce your hero while also bringing the background to life.

This piece started with a question: What would unsaid thoughts look like?

→ **A quilt story**

Better not said

You know how it sounds right? It's that voice inside that calls out your truth but in a whispering tone that only you hear.

I've been thinking about what we don't say

When asked how we are doing, we say *fine* or *good* or *great*. Expressing something more detailed, disturbing or tedious would be surprising. There are some topics that are touchy no matter the audience. When we are in a group of strangers, it's difficult to talk about abortion, racism, immigration or politics because we might step on some beliefs.

We send out little hints in polite company, feeling out which side of the great divides we are on before revealing our position. We use code words to express our dislike. In the South, it is *bless her heart* for someone who is hopelessly wrong or clueless.

We all keep our thoughts to ourselves while navigating conversations. It's a language only we understand. Holding back can foster a peaceful co-existence.

Yet I wondered what holding back does to our consciousness. How does NOT saying something affect what I believe to be true? How does NOT saying something create a tacit understanding among community members of where I stand? How does NOT saying something affect my inner peace? Does saying my truth out loud create barriers or bridges?

I'm all over the place with this. It's hard to even write what I mean here.

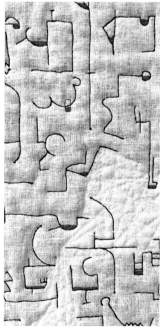

Sandwiching dark fabric behind the foreground linen gave me a shape to react to. Adding red stitching to the shapes gave me a way to illustrate the things we hold back—the words we do not voice.

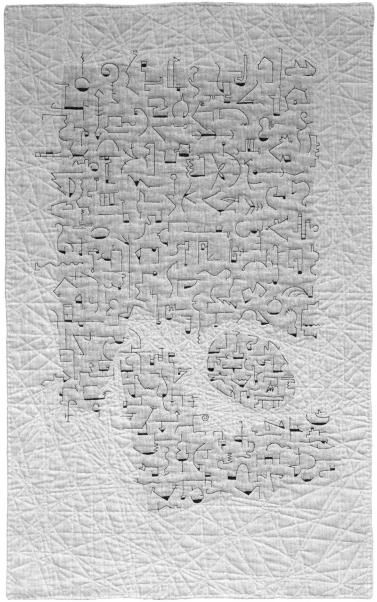

Better Not Said, 41" x 26.5", 2019
Notice how the background fill uses the process I call Heroes, described on page 24. The white-on-white stitching goes up to the hero spaces and then bounces to another edge. I call this ricochet stitching. It gives an overall active texture and contrasts with the organic shapes stitched into the darker area.

thoughts from my journal

Why quilting?

Why do I use fabric and thread? I like the texture, line quality and meditative space it requires. It also refer-ences time, tradition and craftsmanship. All mediums are valid; some feel nubbier, take more time and chal-lenge the viewer to explore the surface of meaning.

For me, quilting takes ideas and breathes a new level of meaning into them.

insights?

I am inspired by reading. It feeds my inner voice and gives my artwork ballast. Once inspired I know that my mind will not rest until I have worked things out in stitch.

Sometimes my best inspiration comes from the fabric, and I need to start stitching to figure out what I'm going to do next. I often put small pieced samples up on my design wall where I can see them every day, and wait for the fabric to tell me what it wants to do.

Some people like to plan out their quilts in detail before they get started; others like to start sew-ing things together and see what happens. Some people get their main inspiration from photos or sketches from nature; some are inspired by a word, a phrase, a concept, a book; others are inspired by choosing a palette of fabrics from their stash. Some people like to work in silence, others like to listen to music or audio books or watch TV.

Now it's your turn

What inspires you? What steps do you take to process ideas?

_____

_____

_____

_____

_____

_____

_____

_____

_____

_____

_____

_____

_____

_____

_____

_____

_____

_____

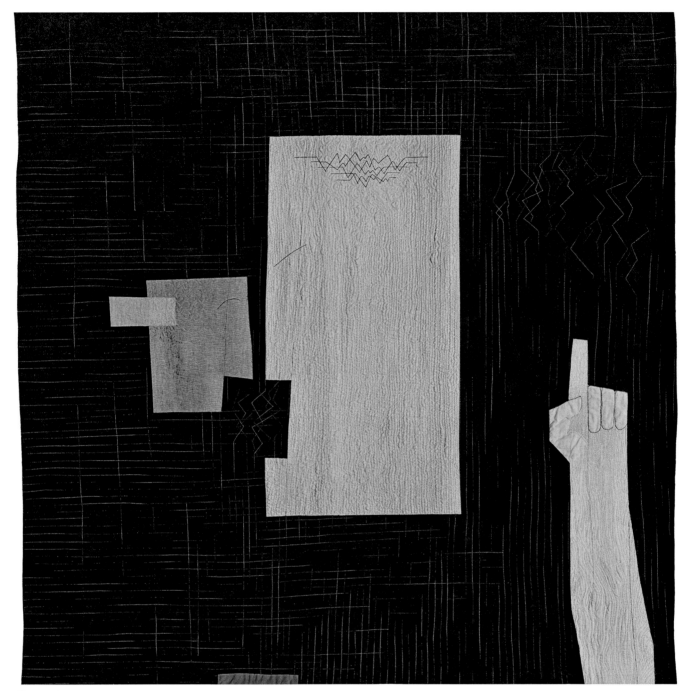

Quilts communicate

I made this piece back in 2011. It was done in response to the talking heads I was watching on TV. It is called *Pundit*. As political discourse heats up, pundits fuel the fire.

As I approached this piece, I was determined to make a statement—like a graphic poster. The large talking head in the composition dominates an imagined conversation while the smaller head tries to keep an open mind.

Talking heads are still telling us what to think. I'm hoping that soon the discourse will cool down and turn into dialogue.

Using a variegated black-to-white thread on black fabric gave me a woven texture that holds these figures in space. Simple line changes imply voices and movement.

Pundit, 41.5" x 41.5", 2011

Edginess

I've been thinking about edges today—how they define differences, beginnings, decisions and boundaries. How the term "edgy" feels uncomfortable on my skin. How edginess often helps me push on but at the same time reels me in.

I'm one of those people who, when confronted with the edge of a cliff, cling to the nearest tree. Others are at the edge peering into the unknown. No, not me. Edges are too scary. I know that I will be tumbled into the abyss by the slightest breeze.

Art is all about the edges. And sometimes I am, in fact, tumbling. I want to navigate the journey and trust myself to navigate well. When doubt settles in, I have to punch through. Inner dialogue is easily obscured by outer pretense. Bare naked exposure makes my skin crawl and my thoughts scramble. Am I really showing my truth? Or is this an exercise in mending?

Sitting down with needle ready makes the silence roar. The edge is near. Sometimes I have to tie it down in a neat and syncopated rhythm. Other times I let the static in and the edges feel like the needles. Hairs on end.

The edges of this hole in a sycamore tree beckon curious creatures. There is darkness within, most likely harboring life.

Edges of thoughts can be raw, jagged and tongue-tied.

"I want to stay as close to the edge as I can without going over. Out on the edge you see all kinds of things you can't see from the center."

- Kurt Vonnegut

Standing above this puddle gives me the feeling that I could dive into a separate reality. The edges here are about perception versus reality.

Symbols as proxy for text

Symbols play a huge role in the everyday understanding of our world. They simplify larger concepts, bring unity to community and deepen the mysterious. They can also be used as a personal tool to communicate without words. It's no surprise that corporations brand their products and services with symbols. Used correctly these visual symbols can be powerful substitutes for text.

Think about the symbols in your life and how they represent you. Experiment with how those symbols might be stitched into your work. Are they rough and obscure or neat and obvious? Can several be combined to speak louder than words or whisper something intimate and personal? Can you create your own personal alphabet?

Add-a-bump

Slow build—echoing and reacting

Learning to react to stitching takes time and focus. Think of it like a story. Each line builds the plot. Each pathway changes the story of the stitch. It's a simple skill that is rewarding in practice. It requires focus and forethought to build a playground for extemporaneous stitching.

First Draw

Using pen and paper or dry erase marker and acetate, draw a line across the bottom of your square. Add another line above it, then another.

Then, add a bump. A bump is anything you want: a simple geometric shape, a floral element, a facial profile—you choose. Subsequent lines echo and react to the line before.

Then Stitch

Repeat the drawing exercise with stitch. The bumps become active players in your story. Each stitching line reacts to the bumps, builds on the action and adds to the plot of the story. The drama builds or becomes calmer. Characters in your story come into focus—or politely disappear.

This add-a-bump sketch shows how the transition between each line level adds drama and excitement to the composition. Each line reacts to the previous line. Bumps can be anything—a zig after a zag, a hill after a valley, or a repeating element that is echoed line by line.

Sometimes stitching an add-a-bump sequence is easier if I turn my square 90 degrees and stitch up and down rather than left to right. Try both ways to see what works for you.

I can't draw!

For me, the solution is always draw what you can, not what you can't. If you aren't Leonardo, don't try to be Leonardo.

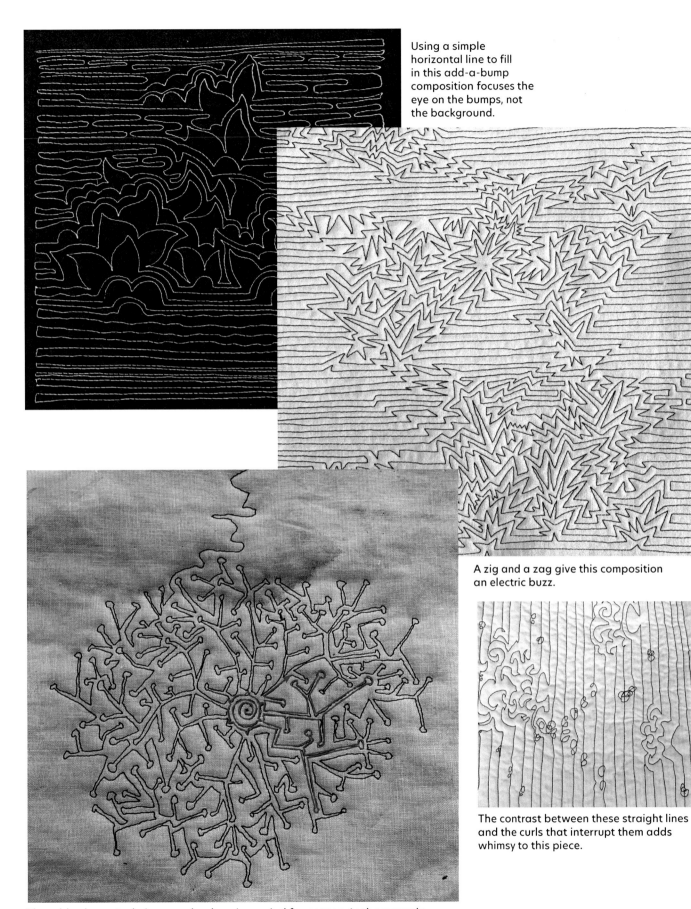

Using a simple horizontal line to fill in this add-a-bump composition focuses the eye on the bumps, not the background.

A zig and a zag give this composition an electric buzz.

The contrast between these straight lines and the curls that interrupt them adds whimsy to this piece.

The add-a-bump technique can be done in a spiral format too. In the example above, the stitching starts in the center with a spiral (see the red line showing the beginning of my path) then a few tiny bumps, then a big complex bump with lots of arms jutting off. When it returns to the center, the pathway continues counterclockwise, making more complex arms.

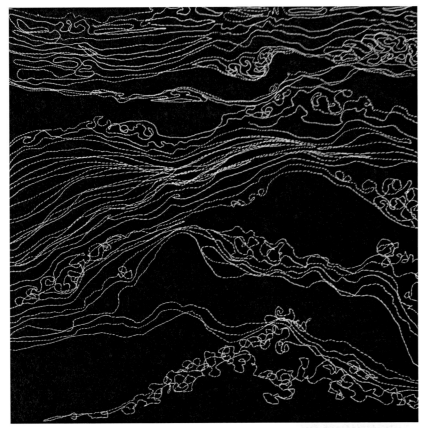

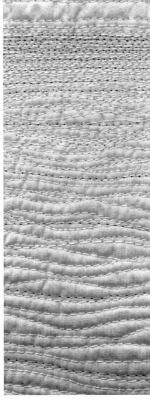

Using a variegated thread and changing the density of the stitching can change the color and texture of the cloth. Notice that in many places on this piece I crossed over adjacent lines to create a denser texture in some areas.

Bubbles and froth stitched with white thread on black fabric.

This white-on-white stitching in the add-a-bump technique gave me a sky for my antennas.

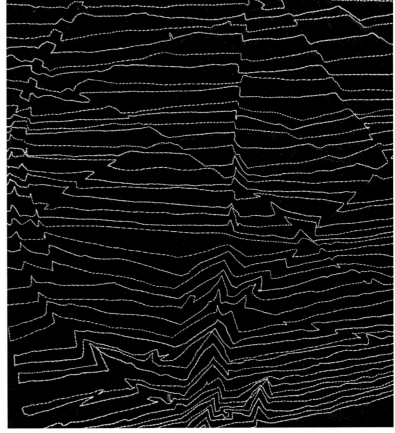

This add-a-bump study reminds me of earthquake fracture lines.

Step by step

This quilt started with a drawing of rounded shapes. I was thinking about how we store memories and how images can bring up powerful thoughts.

I experimented with color, techniques and density before moving on to fabric and thread.

I used a scalloped-edge tablecloth, folded in half, with some batting sandwiched between the two layers for my surface. I then stitched the shapes onto the cloth. Some shapes were recognizable objects, others were abstract blobs. They fit into each other like a puzzle.

Each shape required that I bury the thread ends into the batting. I used a self-threading needle to capture the threads on the front of the quilt, inserted the needle at their base, and pulled them to the back of the quilt. The ends were tied together in a simple knot then, using the self-threading needle again, I pulled the thread ends into the batting layer of the quilt and snipped off the ends.

To add subtle color, I defined circular areas with a light pencil and stitched a dense fill.

Original drawing with pen and paper.

Another version using watercolor

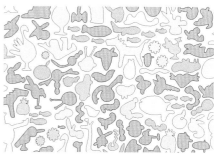

Yet another version experimenting with a repeat pattern in a digital format.

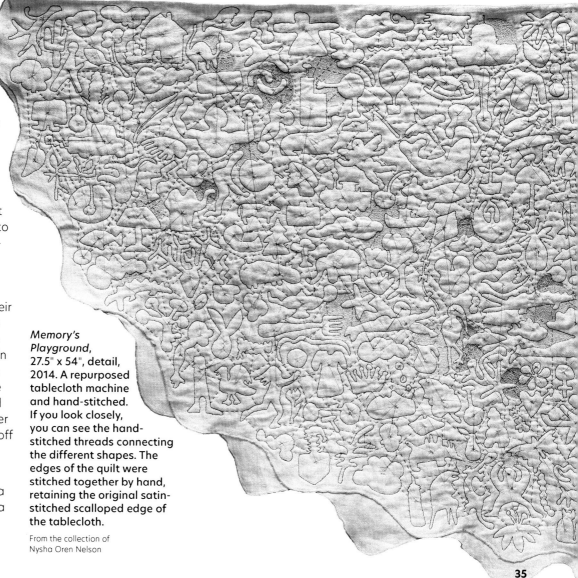

Memory's Playground, 27.5" x 54", detail, 2014. A repurposed tablecloth machine and hand-stitched. If you look closely, you can see the hand-stitched threads connecting the different shapes. The edges of the quilt were stitched together by hand, retaining the original satin-stitched scalloped edge of the tablecloth.

From the collection of Nysha Oren Nelson

→ **A quilt story**

Tuning in to outside influences

Taste buds do it. Ear worms do it. Lurking scents do it. Words do it. Dreams do it.

Knowledge Has Raw Edges began with a pieced top that failed.

Stacking squares of fabric was like assembling a puzzle.

If I see a picture of french fries, I actually taste them. Play a Joni Mitchell song for me and I will hum it for weeks. If I smell Old Spice aftershave, I think of my father. If I see a drawing that speaks to me, I'll find hints of it in my stitching. I think one of the reasons I make art is to catalog all of the influences in my life. I want to leave a record of my thoughts.

Last year, I read a book about the biography of cancer, a second book about the biome of bacteria we live among and a third book about the millions of people who were in the "New" world before the Europeans arrived.

Their stories and how the explorers and scientists of today are unearthing new truths bring light to subjects that are often obscured. (See the list of books below.)

These nonfiction books make me think. They bring up ideas that I didn't have before reading them. They turn on the receptors in my brain, enliven my curiosity and add to the library of imagery that I incorporate into my work. The piece pictured here is an example of that.

Nonfiction changes the way I work

The pieced top shown above was on my design wall for a number of months. I didn't finish it because it didn't have any meaning to me. It was just a pretty picture. I liked the colors but not the layout. It lacked something important.

After reading these three books, I was thinking about specimens and trial balloons, invasive cellular growth, archaeological layers and population centers, and I decided to reflect these ideas in reconstructing the quilt.

I cut the quilt top into 1.5" squares so that I could start fresh. I stacked the tiny pieced squares with more squares of contrasting fabric, then stabilized each of the stacks onto a larger backing with a spot of glue so that I could begin overstitching. It was a mistake. The glue changed the color of the fabric and looked like I had stained the fabric.

Not one to waste an opportunity, I decided to outline each stain—as if I were identifying bacteria on a slide or pinpointing a clay shard in an archaeological dig.

The piece started to take on its own character as I began to identify groupings. I added a rough grid pattern in the light blue squares to imitate data collection.

Recommended reading

The Emperor of All Maladies: A Biography of Cancer, Siddhartha Mukherjee

Never Home Alone: From Microbes to Millipedes, Camel Crickets, and Honeybees, the Natural History of Where We Live, Rob Dunn

1491: New Revelations of the Americas Before Columbus, Charles C. Mann

I am receptive and susceptible to outside influences. It is often beyond my control.

Adding rough circles of stitch to hold down each of the layered squares of fabric creates an implied pattern and extra texture.

I added detail to some of the stains to identify differences.

The edges are flapping off the background on purpose. I loved how they added action to the piece. I put the piece into the dryer after wetting it down to fluff it up and fray it more.

Look for the final quilt on my website: paulakovarik.com

Knowledge Has Raw Edges, 26.25" x 33", 2019

Adding a grid to each of the light blue squares adds a new layer of depth to the piece.

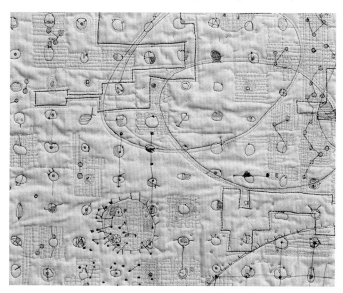

The back of the piece shows just how much extra stitching I added.

practice

Have you read a book that brought new insights? Or a podcast that became a tickling memory? Do you take the time to jot down notes that you want to remember? Is there a detail that intrigues you about a character, a plot or a setting that will spur an idea for a new piece of work?

Take the time to notice something about a book, podcast, movie or TV show. Use a simple note for things you want to remember. Make a rough sketch of a setting or a short quote of dialogue.

Some of my favorite books

Mink River, Brian Doyle

The Book of Delights: Essays, Ross Gay

The Glory and the Dream, William Manchester

The Overstory, Richard Powers

Life After Life, Kate Atkinson

Late Migrations: A Natural History of Love and Loss, Margaret Renkl

Homegoing, Yaa Gyasi

Some of my favorite podcasts

TED talks

This American Life

Stuff You Should Know

Radio Lab

On Being

The Moth

Serial

Invisibilia

Hidden Brain

One-line drawings

The bag on the left is a raw muslin bag that needed some decoration so I used a permanent marker to do a one-line drawing on it. The little bag on the right is made of a practice square that had one-line stitching on it.

A meditation

Pen, paper, distraction. No expectations. Play with the character of line. Does any of this fit into my work? What happens if I use these ideas with stitch? These are the questions I ask myself while drawing.

Stitching is often one continuous line. Stopping and starting begets loose ends that have to be tied and buried. I draw lines that are continuous so that my hands and eyes get the practice I need to stitch later. I use the drawings as starting points and refer to them while stitching on scraps of fabric.

Try this:

1. **Start with pen and paper.** Begin a drawing at any point on your page. Do not lift the pen off the paper.

2. **Draw one continuous line.** Let the pen tell you where it wants to go. Fill the page. Think about textures you have seen, images you want to incorporate, rhythm you want to establish. Try drawing in response to music.

3. **Stitch.** Take out one of your practice squares and start stitching. Play with different-sized shapes, different line attributes. Let the stitch lead.

The little drawing at left inspired this quilt, *Looking for Love in all the Wrong Places*, 44" x 44", detail, 2012. Yes, that black stitching is all one line.

Building stitch

Some examples

Think about stitching as an additive element. In other words, start with a structure and then enhance it by adding other textures. Layering color and texture into your compositions through stitch can be done by machine or hand stitching. This example shows a one-line design that was then textured and enhanced by other stititching.

It's Complicated, 66" x 23", detail, 2020

If you follow this black line, you can see how I travel across the piece while reacting to what was there before.

Echoing the black one-line design with blue, orange, yellow and gray thread adds color to the composition.

Tone-on-tone horizontal stitching adds texture without adding detail and unifies the negative spaces.

Defining shapes behind the foreground images in a soft gray fill can highlight and add depth to the subject in a subtle way.

A hand-stitched grid of dots defines this space.

The composition had some areas that were open enough to add other figures to the piece.

Sprinkling in machine-stitched dots of color can add sparkle to an area.

This layered stitching is perfect for a composition entitled *Chaos Ensues*, detail.

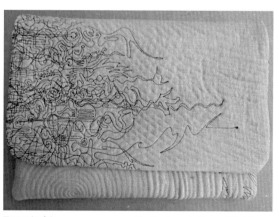

Try stitching over an area that already has stitching on it. Sometimes that extra texture can be a good contrast to a simply stitched background.

Layered stitching helps define these characters and their demeanor.

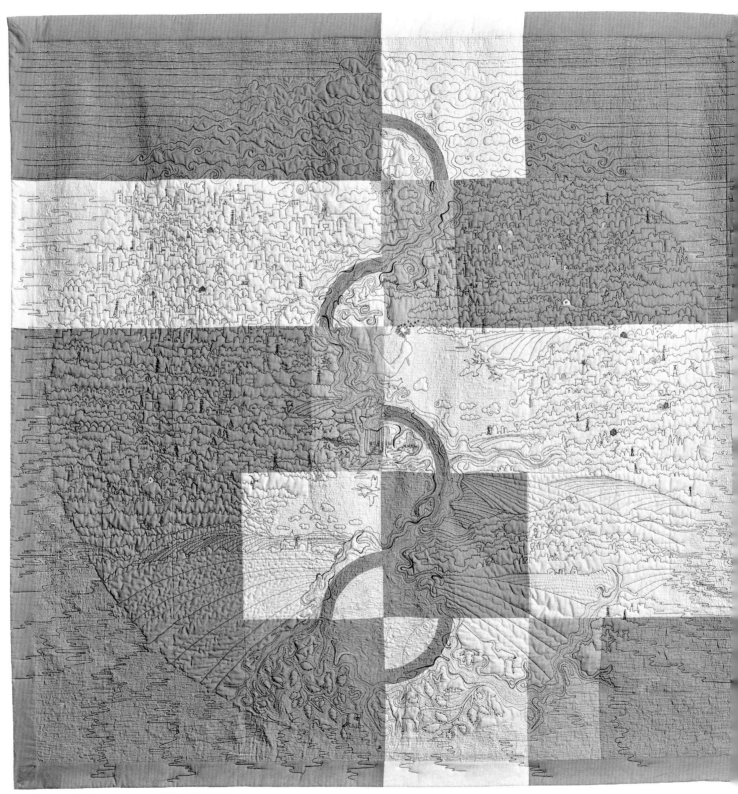

Stream of Consequences, 71" x 71", 2012

Relief and resolution

In 2012, I was invited to participate in a Studio Art Quilt Associates show entitled Earth Stories. The quilt needed to be 72" x 72" and devoted to an organization that was doing good work for our environment. I chose the Wolf River Conservancy, an agency that is protecting a waterway that snakes through our city. The pictures on the right show some of the stages for the original version of *Stream of Consequences,* a quilt that had to be scrapped. Here's what I had to say when I decided to start over:

> Spent yesterday deciding to scrap about eight weeks of work on this piece. Angst, terror, relief, joy and trepidation pushed me toward the decision. How could I possibly give up? Why spend so much time on something that is not working? Am I overthinking? Where is the piece taking me? Why do I feel like I am swimming upstream on it? Maybe if I spend a few more hours working on it I can salvage it?
>
> No.
>
> It was clear that I was making it worse. The stitching competed with the fabrics, the composition did not hold together and the technical problems obscured the message. So happily, and with a sense of relief, I put down the seam ripper, wadded it up and threw it on the *Let's make some pillows* pile. Because once you cut up a piece into 12" squares and put some extra padding behind it, anything looks good.
>
> I'll start over from scratch.

The result, on the left, is a more ordered and thoughtful composition that speaks to my original intention.

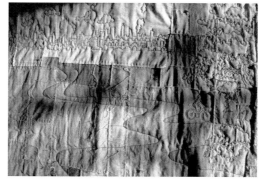

My original idea for this quilt was to use scraps of fabrics attached to a linen backing that could represent the areas of land that were being protected by the Wolf River Conservancy. The Wolf River flows from the countryside through the city. I wanted to show how it connected many different types of land.

I had only a rough plan for how the stitching would intermingle with the scraps. I had lots of photos and sketches of elements that I wanted to include but I didn't have a clear vision of the whole. The stitching was competing with the scraps of fabric and the raw edges were distracting.

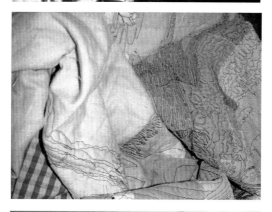

Though I was confident in my idea, the results were getting more and more confused. The story was obscured by the technical problems I was having. This quilt was big. Bigger than my comfort zone and it was difficult to give up on all that work. And I knew that I had no choice. So it was scrapped.

I still have scraps of this quilt hanging around my studio. I learned a lot from it and don't regret the failure.

Traveling unknown pathways

I was talking to a good friend this weekend about the fact that I can't seem to finish things. I am full of ideas and come into the studio each day with a new direction I want to pursue. Exploration, imitation and experimentation all teach me what to do next time—perhaps with a clearer eye to finality. But often that next time doesn't arrive because I'm onto a different idea. A perfect example is this tangent lines piece. It started as an impromptu exploration of color piecing.

I decided to use saturated colors that interact with each other and shatter across a black and white surface. I used an intuitive approach of joining the color pieces from a scrap box instead of pre-planning and cutting to fit.

The composition came together with a strong horizon line and some inter-action between the shapes. I thought it was a good start and that I could play with line to exaggerate a wacky perspective. Since the two colorful figures seemed to be communicating I wanted to emphasize that. I used an acetate overlay and experi-mented with line patterns. I drew plumes of lines coming from the tips of the forms, antennae, perspective lines and heartbeat lines but wasn't happy with any of them.

The piece lingered on the design wall for over a month. Then one day, I came up with the idea of adding a line at each seam that extended across the entire quilt just to see what would happen—an experiment in geometry. Would the composition come together or fall apart? Would the lines impede the message? What message?

This pieced composition started with a bag of scraps.

There were a whole lot of lines to add. Over 275 if I counted right. The texture of the piece changed drasti-cally. The experiment taught me:

- **Lines of sight can be complicated,**
- **Shapes have a presence that might not be apparent to the casual observer,**
- **Interconnectedness can have voids, and**
- **I wasn't sure if I really liked it.**

With nothing to lose, I went for more experimentation.

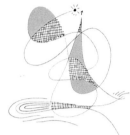

Remember those drawings you did on the back of your math home-work or in your English class spiral note-book where you scribbled a line and then colored the shapes that were formed? I still do that in a vacant sort of doodling mood.

It occurred to me that these lines and forms had even greater secrets to reveal. You know, like a fourth dimen-sion. Perhaps if I colored in areas where the lines formed triangles it would reveal a pattern that connects. Little did I realize that there are over 200 triangles formed by these lines and some of them take a huge hunk of thread to fill in. Tedious. I'm still finding triangles to fill, still seeing triangles in my dreams. Still.

It does give me more ideas to pursue. How do the lines relate to the forms? Where do lines intersect to add more meaning? Why triangles?

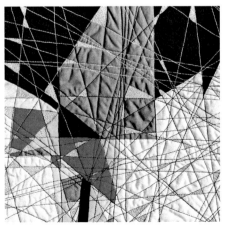

Adding a stitched line at every seam complicated the texture of the piece.

Scrap bag piecing

The nice thing about starting with a scrap bag is the freedom to cut up and reassemble the scraps. Those scraps just don't feel as precious as a new yard of cloth.

Spend a day with a bag of scraps and create a composition that pleases you. It helps if you have a neutral background to anchor the color scraps in space.

Then give it your own *what if* stitching to see what happens. Ask yourself some questions about what the stitching might do. Would a grid of stitches change the dynamic of your composition? How about a floral over-pattern of stitching in a contrasting color? Would some dense fills add interest?

Sightlines, 43" x 19", 2015

From the collection of Kathleen Loomis

Variety, as in: life; spice of

The spicy tang of variety seeped into my studio one week. I work in series. And I work in serious pursuit of message.

Sometimes I grow weary and feel like I am repeating myself. Other times I am overzealous and over my head. This I know: pursuit is the reason. The act of making, stitching, cutting, pressing and assembling fabrics and threads brings clarity to thought. Believe me, if you sit and stitch for three hours on a little scrap of canvas your mind travels, bends and surges.

Here's a little gallery of what I worked on that week:

I finished *Beast*, 44" x 33", 2017. It is a ragged, angry blot that satisfied a certain itch within.

I removed some orange stitching on the center figure of *Thugs*, 35" x 39", detail, 2017. Then added some black flies to the background. Black flies bite.

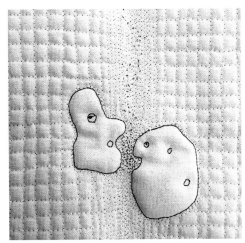

Lots of hand stitching on this little square—part of my Silent Witness series: *Yes, but does it pass the smell test?* 8" x 8", 2017.

This confection of polka dots and swirls satisfied my need to chill out and just let the thread tell me where to go. It's a baby quilt for my niece Willow.

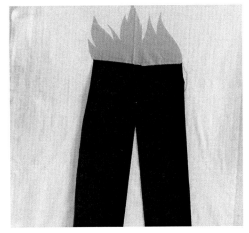

I had an idea of a simple piece after watching alternative facts on the news. I roughed in some fabric pieces for this Pants on Fire idea.

I give myself permission to just have fun sometimes. There is no need to have every piece of work become a masterpiece.

I love how this miniature grid defines a space that is different than the background. Leaving the threads unclipped adds an element of emotion—this guy is really caged in.

Never underestimate the power of a hand-stitched piece. Subtle texturing can be done with tone-on-tone stitching. Stitching with different weights of thread will put emphasis where you want it.

stitch tip

Backing fabrics

Each piece I work on requires a different set of decisions to make. The backing fabric can often be one of the more important ones I have to think about.

When I am assembling pre-stitched pieces of quilts, I often use no backing fabric at all (see page 53 for ideas of how to connect scraps) but more often I use drapery black-out lining as my backing. It stitches like a dream, adds body to the final piece and doesn't stretch. It does, however, add weight.

When I stitch on un-bleached canvas using the one-line technique I often use the same canvas on the back.

Just remember, the backing for your art piece is about creating stability. Any firm stable fabric will do. It will not be seen unless you are intentionally stitching a two-sided art piece.

Deconstruct/reconstruct

I use this mighty tool to deconstruct pieces that no longer speak to me. I look for those quiet ones that seem unbalanced or pretentious. They hide in piles beneath my work table—murmuring.

Some are sharing false narratives. Some seem to be trying too hard. Others just plain bore me. So I get out the rotary cutter and start cutting.

I'll often end up with a pile that stretches to fill my entire work table. I try not to think about how many hours were spent creating the pieces in the first place.

It's about the process, not the product, right?

Then I start stitching again, connecting the diverse pieces to each other by adding another layer of meaning to the story.

This piece, *I Need a Third Eye*, explores the idea that there is so much mystery in life that we need a super power to decipher it all. A third eye would certainly come in handy.

I Need a Third Eye, 45" x 45", 2017 is composed of scraps of pre-quilted fabrics. To get a different perspective on the assembly of these pieces, I stand above the quilt looking down or turn it upside down on my design board to see if it still balances.

After stitching pieces together, I find ways to unify them by overstitching.

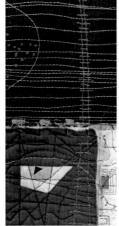

Details entice the viewer to come closer.

When adding stitching to assembled pieces I try to find ways to bring diverse elements together. One stitch pattern will bleed into another and added details will repeat across the piece.

Layering stitch on top of stitching also gives the illusion of depth. The colors blend and a ghost of the previous stitching shows through.

Each piece in this grid has a different texture. Overstitching a curly line unifies the whole.

Yes, I did cut up that quilt

Nothing is precious.
Process beats product.
All is raw material.

If you have been following along with some of the exercises in this book, you will have a number of 14-inch squares with stitching on them. Some are black with white stitching, some are white with black stitching. Some look pretty good, others not so much.

And, since you are browsing through this book I'll bet you have a number of other quilted pieces in your studio that are ready for a face lift. Or, perhaps they need to be recycled and rehabilitated.

This exercise is about letting go.

- **Let go of the legacy.**
- **Let go of the fear.**
- **Let go of the sense that you always have to succeed.**

Nothing is precious.
Process beats product.
All is raw material.

The textures on these quilted pieces invite study and bring a sensual surface to your work. When the pieces are all the same size you can puzzle them together in many ways.

Units made whole again

Here are a few ways to experiment with this process:

1. **Choose a quilt** that is no longer speaking your language. Cut it up into square units and reassemble the squares with a connecting stitch.

2. **Combine two quilts into one.** Choose a common quilt pattern such as Rail Fence, Pinwheel, Log Cabin or Ohio Star. Cut the pattern pieces from your quilted raw material. Butt each piece next to the other and stitch to a background cloth or overstitch across the edges.

3. **Create a collage.** Use some of your sample squares to create an abstract composition. Layer them with other scraps of fabric, or attach them to a base fabric that will add to your composition.

Once the sections are stitched together added stitching will unify the piece. Your overstitching will be different from mine. Developing a vocabulary of stitch designs will come with practice.

Using standard quilt designs with unorthodox materials brings a sense of both organization and chaos.

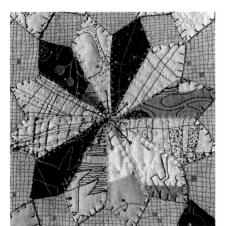

This Dresden Plate variation includes many different scraps of quilts that are stitched together using a decorative machine stitch.

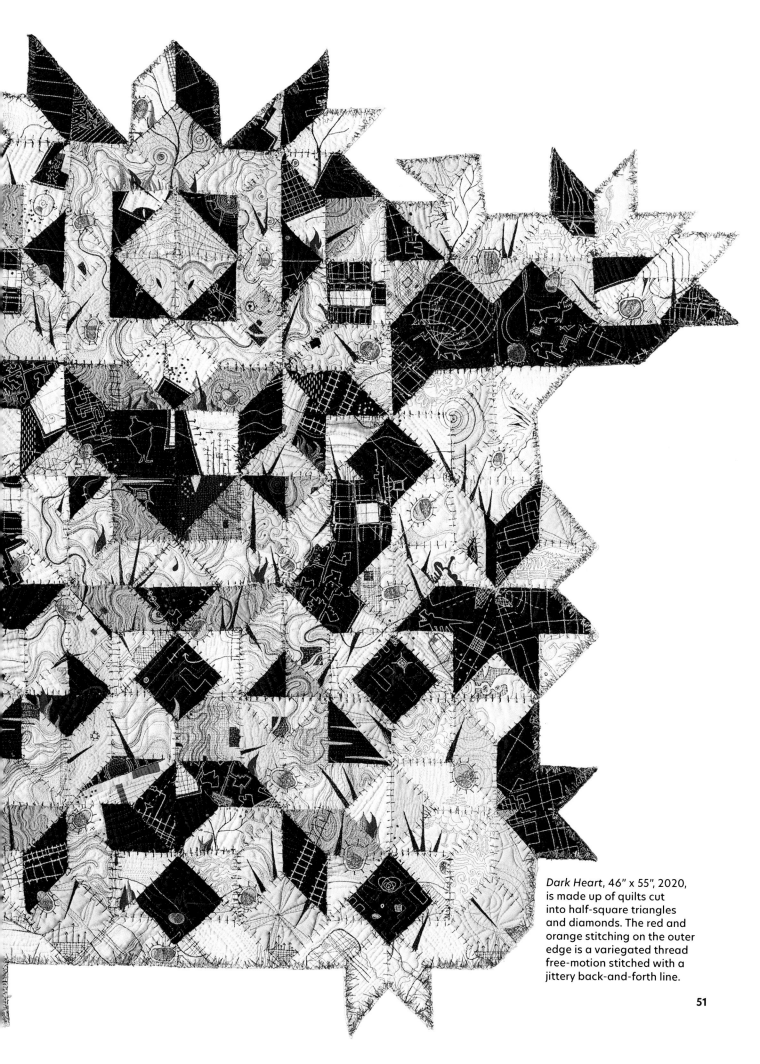

Dark Heart, 46" x 55", 2020, is made up of quilts cut into half-square triangles and diamonds. The red and orange stitching on the outer edge is a variegated thread free-motion stitched with a jittery back-and-forth line.

In the weeds

The original pieced top had some interesting geometric shapes in it that I wanted to emphasize.

I did a lot of stitching on this piece, both by machine and by hand. There was an inkling of dissatisfaction during that time. But my motto tends to be *more is more*, right?

I've been in the weeds about a few things lately. The catharsis of stitching helps me think things out.

For me, working on a quilt is about connection, meditation, intuition and evolution. The work I do is no longer precious, no longer final, no longer static. It lives on, breathes inconsistency and opens new insights. This process keeps me thinking. This process brings pieces together.

The quilt top pictured at left began as an assortment of triangles and rectangles. My thoughts were about sentinels—beings tuned into signals that may not be heard by the rest of us. I worked on it for a few weeks by adding stitching details that connected the geometric shapes.

I let it hang on the studio wall for about a month after that. Then I put it into the divide-and-conquer bin. This piece would not see the light of day until I could resolve its main problems. It was frivolous without a basis in reality. It had an uncomfortable balance. And the wavy surface could not be tamed.

At this point in the project, I realized I was getting nowhere fast.

Then, one day, I had an itch to erase and engage. So I cut it up. I ended up with 96 4" x 4" squares. And it felt really good. Reassembly took a few days. I rearranged and attached the blocks to a backing. I also added a few pieces from other quilts that were in the divide-and-conquer bin.

I am not shy about adding details. I overstitched the squares with new lines that connected some of the textures in each area and added hand-stitched details where I wanted more.

In the Weeds, according to the Cambridge dictionary, means: Concerned with so many problems or so much work that you are finding it difficult to deal with something; or concerned with small details, often when this prevents you from understanding what is important.

The rotary cutter comes out when I realize I am not going to solve problems with a quilt design.

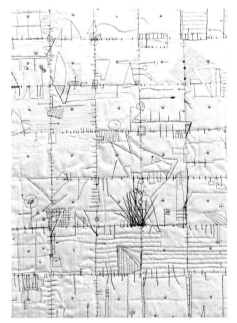

The back of this piece shows how much stitching I added to the existing units. I used my free-motion foot to stitch the scraps to the backing, first by stitching a small dot in the center of each square, then, once stabilized, by stitching the edges.

Connecting the cut-ups

Experimental or unsuccessful quilted pieces are perfect fodder for new work. The texture and line work will add depth to a new composition. I cut them up and reuse them in new work.

Here are some of the ways I have connected the scraps:

- **Butt the pieces side by side and use a decorative stitch** that sutures them together. Make that stitching part of your design or hide it by using a thread color that matches your scraps.

- **Hand stitch the scraps together** to add a detailed and hand-crafted look.

▼ sash

- **Connect the blocks with sashing.** This works well when all your seams are straight. The sashing can complement your scraps or contrast with them.

- **Stitch the scraps to a base fabric.** Any firm fabric will do. The example at left shows how I stabilized my scraps before proceeding. The little orange dots are stitched in the center of each square to keep the square in place.

- **Use a free-motion foot.** A meandering line that connects two scraps together over a base fabric can add to the story of the quilt.

- **Glue the scraps to a base fabric**, then stitch. When using fabric glue, be aware that a little goes a long way.

In the Weeds, 34" x 39.5", 2020

The sentinels are still there but they are more active in their environment. The white squares are unifying the background, creating an environment for the characters within.

The evolution of one piece of work

Back in 2015, I had the opportunity to do an artist residency in the dunes of Lake Michigan. I was captivated by the lake stones. They had personality, presence and power.

Soon after, I started stitching them.

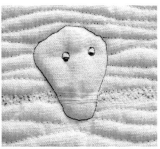

They populated my studio to the point that I had faces looking at me from every corner. So I started putting them together.

The final piece, called *The Secret Life of Stones*, was juried into Quilt National 2017 and traveled for three years.

It came back to me last year and went into storage. I really didn't know what I was going to do with it so I stacked it up with the others and waited until it spoke to me.

When in a cutting up kind of mood, nothing is precious. All things must evolve.

So I cut it up. And made some masks.

It's showing up in other experiments too. Playful things that give me a little laugh during these stressful times.

There are still some scraps to consider. They'll join the rest of the scraps in my scrap box.

Every so often, one or two of them speak to me and give me something else to think about.

Cutting up what is considered precious allows me to let go of the legacy of it and be in the moment. I seek that feeling of exploration and discovery in every work I create.

Using up, re-configuring and re-imagining raw materials can lead to disaster or development. When it is a disaster, I learn. And that's what I am here for—to learn, to excite, to think of alternatives. All things must evolve.

These little constructions are pieces of the *Secret Life of Stones* quilt.

I had this idea that they were trying to tell us something but in a language all their own.

Overlaying a window of the pattern for my mask allowed me to choose the section that I wanted to cut out.

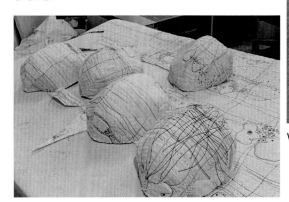

Masks under construction.

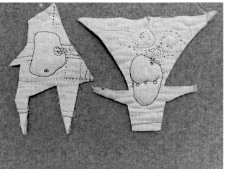

Who doesn't love these two guys?

On evolution

Because I feel that process is more important than the product, I don't allow myself to fall in love with my pieces. Sometimes I abandon one that doesn't seem to be working. Other times I will cut up a finished quilt and reassemble it, maybe combining it with pieces of other quilts. Even if I liked the original quilt, it's always interesting to see how it changes in new configurations.

It's a learning process as well as a way to witness transformation.

Rushing toward stimuli

Preparing chicken soup today, I was chopping onions with the inevitable result of teary eyes. I mentioned this to my grandsons and they both rushed over, one with the scientific explanation of why that was happening and the other eager to chop onions so that he could cry too. We all ended up with wet cheeks and sniffling noses.

The willingness to take a chance or explore uncharted territory is a trait that is tempered with age. Caution sets in. Doubt and preconceived ideas define our comfort map. We stop, look and listen. We teach our kids about the incautious moments of our lives so that they will avoid the shock, hurt or disappointments that we experienced. We put up fences, set up passwords and require more IDs. We box in the acceptable and fence out the challenging.

I'm glad that kids often dismiss what adults say, preferring to experience the thrill of discovery themselves. I once read that to stay young you must remain curious. You must let the onions make you cry.

I will learn from these boys. Oh yes, I will.

Please, pass me some tissue.

stitch tip

Echoing a line

One of my favorite stitching techniques is to echo a line that's already there to add depth to the piece, almost like the lines on a topographical map. Sometimes I place the new line very close to the pre-existing line, maybe even crossing over; sometimes I space the lines more widely (or do both). Sometimes I echo the line in a different color, or several different colors.

My stitching is not perfect; I would probably fail if the quilt police got out their checklists. The number of stitches per inch varies from one place to the next. Some of the lines are wobbly. But I don't worry about that, as long as the stitches add meaning and texture to a piece.

Taking a risk

Back in 2017 I had the opportunity to learn about steamroller printing. I signed up as soon as I heard about it. Each student in the class was given a 4'x8' MDF plywood sheet to create a woodblock that would be used to print fabric.

We worked three days a week for six weeks on our woodcuts. The board was then inked, covered with fabric, paper, a felt blanket and another board so that a steamroller could roll over it to make a print. My woodblock was about disruptions, so I created a large length of fabric of unmatched scraps, pieced in a haphazard fashion, that could be laid onto the board and receive the printed image.

We were all a bit nervous watching that huge steamroller go over the board but the result was worth it.

I ended up doing three different quilts using the fabrics we printed that day. All of them stitched to within an inch of their lives.

And, here's what I learned.

Run to the new.
Try the bizarre.

Disruption, 90" x 40", detail, 2018

57

Editing is good for the soul

In 2016, I worked for five months on a piece I was calling *Silent Witnesses— Birds*. It was inspired by the birds that hang out on the beach watching humans romp. I wanted to use them as a metaphor for all the wildlife out there being affected by humans. I spent hours drawing the composition, stitching the textural background and harboring a desire to make a strong statement.

And it failed.

Miserably.

Was it too literal? Too centered? Too boring? Too black and white?

Yes it was.

So I cut it up with the faith that if I cut the dang thing up I might find the answer to what went wrong.

I ended up with about eight pieces of textured fabric with scraps of meaning. They'll be jumping off points for new thoughts, relieving me of the burden of seeing the piece day after day taunting me to resolve it. Resolve it I did.

It was a good day.

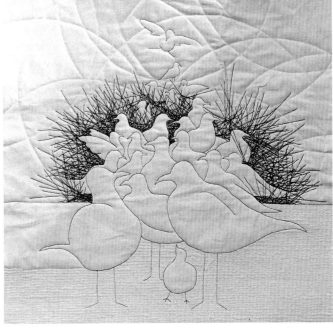

Here's a work-in-progress shot of the piece. The original drawing was from my sketchbook. I transferred the image to the fabric by redrawing it in light pencil. Though I liked what was happening with the background texture, I was unhappy with the way the composition was working. The birds were too flat. The horizon felt too centered and didn't anchor the birds properly in their environment.

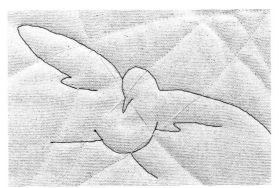

I liked this little bird tied up with thread. As I stitched the background arcs (drawn in chalk on the fabric) I stopped at the bird stitching, moved the quilt under my needle to the other side of his body and started stitching again. The long threads that connect the pieces of the arc make it look like the bird is tied up.

I have used this grass-like texture in many pieces since working on this one. The experiment yielded a new way of thinking about fills.

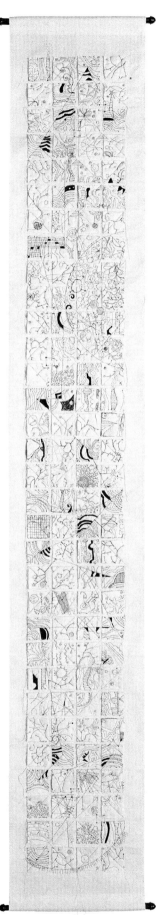

Looking for the Pattern That Connects, 80" x 12.5", 2017

From the collection of Carol Eisenberg

→ **A quilt story**

Still looking

I started this piece with the idea that we search for unifying elements to make sense of chaos. Quilts use repeat modules to create a whole from fragments. So, if I brought disparate elements together, could I create a whole? Here's a few basic thoughts:

- **Regularity unifies.**
- **Grids are glue.**
- **Lines travel and connect.**
- **Connection = comprehension.**

I took a few of the sample thread studies I have lying around and cut them into 2" squares. Assembling them randomly on a background substrate created a tile-like pattern that I emphasized with a 45-degree grid that holds them together.

Then I started looking for connections. These small tiles really have little in common except some black stitching on neutral fabric. My eyes seemed to bounce around the assemblage, hip hopping to find similarities. So I added a line mimicking the hip-hop journey my eyes were taking.

Adding denser fill stitching at the intersections of the connecting line and patterned tile brought a sense of rhythm to the piece.

The front side

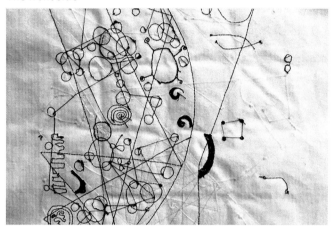

The back side

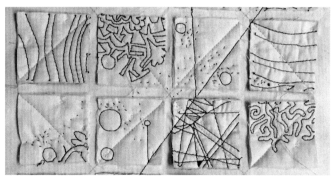

These tiles had little in common, black thread on a neutral background. The 45-degree pink stitching brought them together.

Adding hand-stitched details enhanced the action and brought the tiles together in small areas.

Then I turned the piece to the back to see what was happening with the additional stitching.

The front side is dense with stitching and line work that represents my idea of complexity and chaos.

The back shows a simpler yet texturally consistent stitching that appeals to me. It is raw and random. There's a sense of space on that side that shows the tenuous pathways of connections.

When is enough enough?

I stitch a lot. And I have a lot of raw materials to work with.

So I do. I stitch.

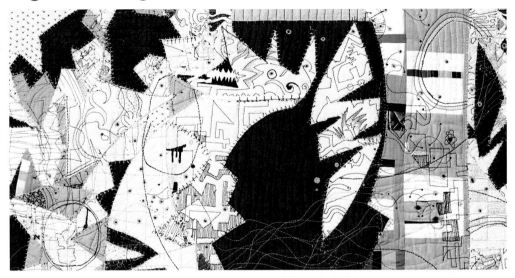

In this exercise, a number of the scraps I had lying around looked like leaves. The toothy quality of those scraps gave me a starting point. I had the idea of creating a jungle of objects.

After assembling the scraps, I overstitched the units to make them more consistently textured. Overstitching the already quilted pieces adds action to the piece and connects disparate elements.

In every project there comes a time when I have to ask myself *when is enough enough?* I admit that this texture looks wacko. I mean it to be disturbing and frantic. My stitching is taking a journey through chaos.

Texture rules here. The hand and machine stitching brings a level of detail worth lingering over.

But does extra detail bring coherence? Am I channeling this confusion to release tension? All I know is that it just feels right to me. **And that's enough.**

We Don't Really Know, Do We? 27" x 33", 2020

practice

Spend some time stitching without planning.

Some of that texture you generate leads you to a new way of thinking.

Choose some quilted scraps with different qualities. Butt the edges together and stitch them with a decorative stitch to bind the edges. Overstitch new details on top of the existing pieces to create a layered effect of pattern and detail. Experiment with different colors or weights of threads.

Some last thoughts

I am at the stage in my career as an artist where I question why. Why do I spend hours linking pieces of fabric with thread? Why does this medium work better than others for my artwork?

I know one thing for sure. I can't NOT do it. The work allows me time to consider this space and time in which we live, time to meditate, time to express my thoughts through intimate detail.

I believe in the power of thought and art. I think the work lives on even if never seen. I once read a quote from Lidewij Edelkoort, who curated a fiber exhibit in Israel. It goes like this:

"We are an unstitched society suffering from a lasting socio-economic crisis that has made us ferociously protective and egocentric. It is time for mending and gathering, thus restoring the fabric of society: picking up the pieces and bringing them together in a patch-work of possibility; a quilt of substance, able to absorb shock and fear."

Art brings beauty and depth to our lives. It tracks the un-spoken, reveals miracles and records time. The mysteries we seek to unravel are only uncovered through long and focused thought and practice. And this medium allows for that.

I know these things:

You have to practice.

You have to make a mess.

You have to feel the depth.

Then try again.

It's process, not product.

So go at it! Stitch some fabric, make some quilts, cut up some quilts and express yourself.

Isolation Chamber, above, 24" x 24" x 24", 2021
What Lies Beneath, on the left, 27" x 21", detail, 2021

I want to hear from you

Though I wish I could be in the same room with each and every one of the artists who are interested in my process, it's just not realistic.

Luckily, we have the internet, and we can share our thoughts and images instantaneously. So share. Show me your practice squares. Send me your thoughts. Tell me what I am missing. Celebrate new insights.

My online journal (**paulakovarik.com/journal**) continues the conversation with myself and others. You can subscribe to receive an email every time I post something.

Or, you can find me on Instagram **@yellowbrickstudio** where I post work-in-progress shots of my art.

Or, send me a note:
atplayinthegardenofstitch@gmail.com

I am always happy to hear from you.

Grateful Grateful Grateful

For my husband, Jim, who encourages my explorations. Our life together has taught me the power of love to transform. Your guidance and encouragement lights the way for my work.

For my family and friends who bring joy and insight to my life. Our gatherings are my best memories, our love gives me hope. I look inside myself through your eyes.

For Kathleen Loomis, whose tireless pursuit of meaning in her work brings depth and inspiration to mine. Your patient review of this book has polished the raw.

For my students who teach me something new every time I have the opportunity to be with them. I celebrate your curiosity.

Made in United States
North Haven, CT
10 February 2025

65703959R00035